TURKEY HUNTING

BY SARA GREEN

BELLWETHER MEDIA • MINNEAPOLIS, MN

Jump into the cockpit and take flight with Pilot books. Your journey will take you on high-energy adventures as you learn about all that is wild, weird, fascinating, and fun!

This edition first published in 2014 by Bellwether Media, Inc.

No part of this publication may be reproduced in whole or in part without written permission of the publisher. For information regarding permission, write to Bellwether Media, Inc., Attention: Permissions Department, 5357 Penn Avenue South, Minneapolis, MN 55419.

Library of Congress Cataloging-in-Publication Data

Green, Sara, 1964-
  Turkey Hunting / by Sara Green.
    pages cm. – (Pilot: Outdoor Adventures)
  Includes bibliographical references and index.
  Summary: "Engaging images accompany information about turkey hunting. The combination of high-interest subject matter and narrative text is intended for students in grades 3 through 7"– Provided by publisher.
  ISBN 978-1-62617-086-5 (hardcover : alk. paper)
  1. Turkey hunting–Juvenile literature. I. Title.
  SK325.T8G74 2014
  799.2′4645–dc23
                    2013036482

Printed in the United States of America, North Mankato, MN.

TABLE OF CONTENTS

A PRIZE GOBBLER

The morning sun rises over the woods. A hunter crouches next to a tree. He stays very still and listens carefully. Suddenly, he hears muffled yelps. These are the sounds made by turkeys roosting in the trees above him. The hunter slips a diaphragm call into his mouth. He uses it to make purrs, clucks, and other hen sounds to attract a gobbler.

Soon, he hears the flap of wings. A turkey lands on the ground in front of him. It is a large gobbler! The turkey struts toward the hunter with his tail feathers fanned out. The hunter slowly raises his shotgun, takes aim, and pulls the trigger. A shot blasts through the air and the gobbler falls. The hunter's aim was perfect! As he carries the gobbler to his truck, he thinks about his evening meal. Wild turkey is definitely on the menu!

Double the Fun

Most animals can only be hunted in the fall, but many states allow turkey hunting in both fall and spring. Often, hunters will hunt turkeys in spring and focus on other game in the fall.

Every spring and fall, hunters head outdoors to search for wild turkeys. Turkey hunting is a challenging activity. Turkeys have keen hearing and vision. These cautious game birds flee from unusual noises and sights. Hunters use patience and skill to outsmart the turkeys.

Wild turkeys travel in small flocks. They are often found in wooded habitats near meadows and clearings. During the day, they search for food in open areas. They roost in trees at night for protection. Wild turkeys change locations depending on the time of year and where food is available. Hunters study the habits of turkeys to learn where to hunt them. Often, hunters will scout roosting spots the night before a hunt. They return to these places before sunrise the next morning. When the turkeys fly down from the trees, the hunters are ready to shoot.

ON THE HUNT

Most turkey hunters use shotguns to shoot turkeys. They often carry guns that have a **camouflage** finish. Hunters load shotguns with **cartridges**. These shells are filled with small pellets called shot. When the hunter pulls the trigger, the shot blasts through the air toward the target. Hunters aim for the neck and head of the turkey. This keeps shot out of the part of the turkey that people like to eat.

cartridge

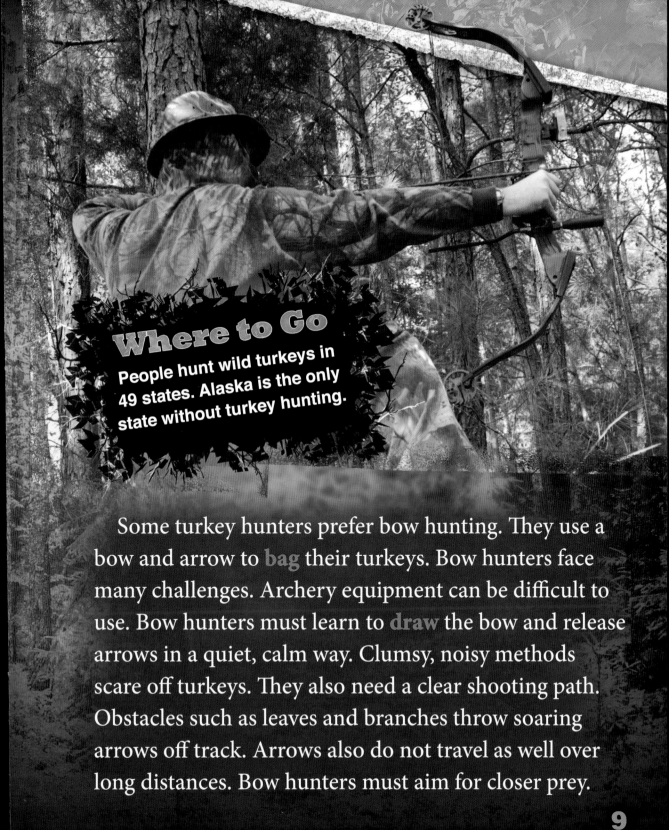

Where to Go

People hunt wild turkeys in 49 states. Alaska is the only state without turkey hunting.

Some turkey hunters prefer bow hunting. They use a bow and arrow to bag their turkeys. Bow hunters face many challenges. Archery equipment can be difficult to use. Bow hunters must learn to draw the bow and release arrows in a quiet, calm way. Clumsy, noisy methods scare off turkeys. They also need a clear shooting path. Obstacles such as leaves and branches throw soaring arrows off track. Arrows also do not travel as well over long distances. Bow hunters must aim for closer prey.

Turkey hunters wear special clothing to trick turkeys. Camouflage facemasks, caps, gloves, and other clothing help them blend with the woods. Hunters wear boots to protect their feet in rugged or wet terrain. Waterproof pants keep hunters comfortable in the rain. Hunters are often outdoors for long hours. They dress in layers to stay comfortable as temperatures change. Many carry camouflaged daypacks to store extra clothing.

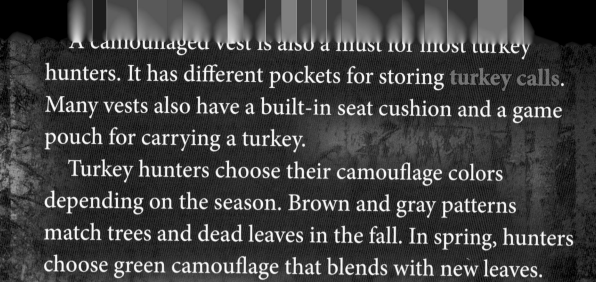

A camouflaged vest is also a must for most turkey hunters. It has different pockets for storing turkey calls. Many vests also have a built-in seat cushion and a game pouch for carrying a turkey.

Turkey hunters choose their camouflage colors depending on the season. Brown and gray patterns match trees and dead leaves in the fall. In spring, hunters choose green camouflage that blends with new leaves.

Turkey hunters imitate the natural sounds of turkeys to lure them into shooting range. Some use their voices. Most use turkey calls. **Friction calls** are among the most popular. To use these, hunters rub two surfaces together to make turkey sounds. One of the simplest is the **box call**. This is a small wooden box with a lid. To make the call, hunters rub the lid against the top edge of the box. Hunters with advanced calling skills use diaphragm calls. Hunters inhale and exhale through devices in their mouth to make turkey sounds.

Skilled hunters use different calls depending on the situation. Some calls help hunters locate turkeys. Others draw turkeys out of hiding. Hunters listen to recordings of turkeys to learn their yelps, clucks, purrs, and other sounds. Then they practice making the calls. The calls must sound real or the turkeys will run away.

box call

decoy

Many turkey hunters use decoys to attract turkeys. The simplest decoys are made of cardboard or fabric. More realistic ones are made of foam or plastic. Some are even covered with feathers and have moving heads. Hunters often set hen and jake decoys near each other. When a jealous gobbler runs out to chase away the jake, the hunter is ready to shoot.

Many states allow turkey hunters to use dogs, especially during the fall season. The dogs help hunters locate a flock of turkeys. Then the dogs run through the flock, barking loudly. The turkeys fly off in all directions. However, turkeys do not stay scattered for long. They will regroup as a flock. The hunters wait for the turkeys' return with their weapons ready. While the hunters wait, the dogs know to rest quietly. Some even curl up in camouflaged bags to sleep.

Fast Movers

Wild turkeys can fly for short bursts at speeds up to 55 miles (89 kilometers) per hour. They can run at speeds up to 25 miles (40 kilometers) per hour.

RESPONSIBILITY AND SAFETY

Hunting carries a lot of responsibility. Hunters who behave recklessly can injure themselves or others with their weapons. Turkey hunters can prevent accidents by following important safety rules. They treat every gun as if it is loaded. This means they never point it at another person. They must never shoot until they see the entire turkey. Other hunters making calls and rustling in the trees may be mistaken for real turkeys.

Hunters also must make themselves known to other hunters. They do this in several ways. They should wear blaze orange when walking in the woods. They should never wear colors associated with a turkey, such as red, blue, or white. These are the colors of a gobbler's head. After collecting a dead turkey, a hunter should wrap it with a blaze orange ribbon or place it in a long zippered bag. This way, another hunter will not mistake it for a live turkey and shoot at it.

The Four Rules of Firearm Safety:

1. Treat every firearm as if it is loaded.

2. Point guns in a safe direction. Never point a firearm at yourself or others.

3. Keep your finger off the trigger until you are ready to fire.

4. Be sure of your target and beyond. Make sure you positively identify what you are shooting at. Also know what lies in front of and beyond it.

All turkey hunters must purchase a license and follow state hunting laws. Each state limits the number of turkeys a hunter can kill. Some states only allow spring hunting, while others have both spring and fall seasons. Fall hunters can bag both male and female turkeys. Spring hunters can only shoot gobblers and jakes. They must leave the hens alone to lay eggs and raise their young. Turkey hunters always identify a turkey's gender before they pull the trigger.

Responsible turkey hunters respect the land. They take all trash and equipment home after they finish hunting. They also ask permission from landowners before hunting on private land. Many turkey hunters join groups to help conserve turkey habitats. Their efforts help increase turkey populations and keep them healthy. Hunters who care about the land ensure that others will have the opportunity to hunt turkeys for years to come.

TURKEY HUNTING IN ALABAMA

One of the best states for hunters to bag wild turkeys is Alabama. For decades, people living in Alabama worked hard to improve turkey habitats and raise numbers. Today, Alabama's piney woods and swamps host plenty of wild turkeys. The state is now home to around 500,000 wild turkeys. This is one of the highest populations in the nation.

Alabama turkey hunters also enjoy one of the longest hunting seasons in the country. Every year, around 60,000 wild turkeys are bagged. Each hunter is allowed to shoot five turkeys per year. Most states only allow one or two. Many hunters like the challenge of hunting on public land, such as national forest land. Others trek across private land with experienced guides. Either way, Alabama turkey hunters can look forward to heart-pounding fun in beautiful scenery.

It's Official!

In 1980, the wild turkey was named Alabama's official game bird.

GLOSSARY

bag—to shoot down and capture

box call—a turkey call that makes sound by rubbing a lid against the top edge of a box

camouflage—a specific pattern meant to blend in with natural surroundings

cartridges—shells that contain everything needed to fire shot from a shotgun

conserve—to protect; hunters conserve turkey habitats so they will always have somewhere to hunt.

decoys—life-like models of birds; hunters use decoys to attract real birds.

diaphragm call—a turkey call that makes sound by placing a device in the mouth and inhaling or exhaling

draw—to bend a bow by pulling the string

friction calls—turkey calls that make sounds by rubbing two parts of a device together

game—wild animals hunted for food or sport

gobbler—an adult male turkey; gobblers are also called toms.

hen—a female turkey

jake—a young male turkey

keen—sharp

license—a document that gives legal permission to do an activity

roosting—settling together in a group to rest

scout—to explore an area to learn more about it

terrain—the surface features of an area of land

turkey calls—noisemakers that mimic the sounds a turkey makes; turkey calls are used to attract turkeys.

TO LEARN MORE

At the Library

MacRae, Sloan. *Turkey Hunting*. New York, N.Y.: PowerKids Press, 2011.

Omoth, Tyler. *Turkey Hunting for Kids*. North Mankato, Minn.: Capstone Press, 2013.

Pound, Blake. *Duck Hunting*. Minneapolis, Minn.: Bellwether Media, 2013.

On the Web

Learning more about turkey hunting is as easy as 1, 2, 3.

1. Go to www.factsurfer.com.

2. Enter "turkey hunting" into the search box.

3. Click the "Surf" button and you will see a list of related Web sites.

With factsurfer.com, finding more information is just a click away.

INDEX